KINDERGARTEN READING COMPREHE

GW01454404

My name: _____

Color a star each time you read the story.

I can read about…

Jim and Kim Go Fast

Jim and Kim get in the car.

The car is big and red.

Jim says go. Kim hits the gas.

Jim and Kim go fast! Jim says

What color is the car?	◯ black
Who hits the gas?	◯ Jim
What does Jim say first?	◯ go

Write the word.

Talk Abo
(Parents, ask your child t

Why do you t

My name: _____

Color a s
you re

I can read about…

The Sun

The sun is up in the sky.

It is a big yellow star.

The sun is made of hot gas.

Do not look at the sun. It is bad for yo

What is the sun?	◯ a rock	◯ a st
Should you look at the sun?	◯ yes	◯
What is the sun made of?	◯ gas	◯

Color the sun.

Talk About The
(Parents, ask your child these questio

Why shouldn't you look

My name: _____

you read the story.

I can read about…

Max And Dad

Max likes to fish.

His dad likes to fish too.

Max and his dad go to the big lake.

Oh no! The boat will not go!

Who likes to fish?	◯ Mom	◯ Max
The lake is _____.	◯ big	◯ little
Who goes to the lake with Max?	◯ his dad	◯ a pal

Write the word.

Talk About The Text
(Parents, ask your child these questions about the text)

What problem do Max and his dad have?

Contact the author :
fishyrobb.com

ISBN: 979-8-86951496-7

First printing edition 2023.

10 9 8 7 6 5 4 3 2 1

Published in Ormond Beach, Florida.

TABLE OF CONTENTS

How to Use This Book

Learning to read is more than just sounding out words. Children also need to understand the words on the page. This is called reading comprehension.

Reading comprehension begins to develop when children are very small. Listening to a parent read aloud and interacting is when it starts. As little ones learn to sound out words and read on their own, reading comprehension often lags behind – because it's a lot of work just decoding written language!

This workbook is designed to give beginning readers many opportunities to build comprehension skills as they read stories on their level. The sentences are short, simple, and easy to understand with lots of kindergarten-level sight words.

Each story is followed by three comprehension questions for the student plus a picture to color or sight word to trace. Finally, there is a "Talk About the Text" question that provides an opportunity for you and your child to connect with the story.

Best of all, these kindergarten reading passages will allow your child to read confidently and proudly!

It's important not to overwhelm young readers. One story per day is a great place to start. The stories in this book progress in difficulty, so start at the beginning and work back. Most of all, have fun!

This page contains kindergarten level sight words used in the stories. These are words that can not be sounded on phonetically. These word cards can be cut out and used as flashcards.

is	my
to	he
the	she
very	want

my

is

he

to

she

the

want

very

This page contains kindergarten level sight words used in the stories. These are words that can not be sounded on phonetically. These word cards can be cut out and used as flashcards.

put	my
to	blue
does	be
no	go

any

put

blue

to

be

does

This page contains kindergarten level sight words used in the stories. These are words that can not be sounded on phonetically. These word cards can be cut out and used as flashcards.

what	do
your	come
one	two
find	so

what	do
your	come
one	two
find	so

This page contains kindergarten level sight words used in the stories. These are words that can not be sounded on phonetically. These word cards can be cut out and used as flashcards.

her	have
goes	live
me	good
are	says

have

here

live

does

bad

me

save

are

My name: _____

☆ ☆ ☆

I can read about...

My Dog Sam

Sam is my dog.

He likes to play.

Sam has a red ball.

He plays with the red ball.

| Who is Sam? | ◯ my dad | ◯ my dog |

| What does Sam like to do? | ◯ play | ◯ jump |

| What does Sam play with? | ◯ a ball | ◯ a bone |

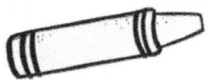

Color Sam's ball.

Talk About The Text
(Parents, ask your child these questions about the text)

Is Sam a girl or a boy?

How do you know?

My name: _____

I can read about...

My Dog Sam

Sam is my dog.

is him to play

Sam has a red ball

play with the red ball

My name: _____

☆ ☆ ☆

I can read about...

Pam's New Pal

Pam has a new pal.

She met her pal at the park.

Pam and her pal run and play.

Pam's new pal is Jen.

Where did Pam meet a pal?	◯ park	◯ school

Who is Pam's pal?	◯ Jim	◯ Jen

What do Pam and her pal do?	◯ run	◯ sit

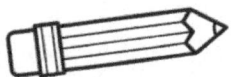

Write the word.

park

Talk About The Text
(Parents, ask your child these questions about the text)

Did the pals have fun?

How can you tell?

My name: _____

☆ ☆ ☆

I can read about...

A Hot Pot

That is a very big pot.

I want to look in the pot.

Stop! That pot is too hot!

Mom put the lid back on top.

Where do I want to look?	◯ in the pot	◯ on a lid
The pot is very _____.	◯ little	◯ big
What did mom put on top?	◯ the lid	◯ the pot

Write the word.

stop [STOP]

Talk About The Text
(Parents, ask your child these questions about the text)

What might have happened
if mom didn't say stop?

19

My name: _____

I can read about...

A Hot Pot

That is a very big pot.

I want to look in the pot.

Stop! That pot is too hot!

Mom put the lid back on top.

My name: _____

Color a star each time you read the story.

I can read about...

My Cat Tab

Tab is my fat black cat.

She likes to sit on the mat.

Tab naps on her mat.

Then Tab will play on the mat.

What is my cat's name? ○ Tab   ○ Tom

Where does Tab nap? ○ in bed   ○ on her mat

What kind of cat is Tab? ○ fun   ○ fat

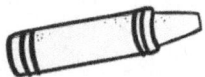 Color Tab.

Talk About The Text
(Parents, ask your child these questions about the text.)

What happens after Tab naps?

How do you know?

21

My name: _____

Color a star each time
you read the story.

⭐ ⭐ ⭐

I can read about...

Mom And Her Van

Mom has a big blue van.

She can go fast in her van.

Six kids can fit in the van.

We ride to school in mom's van.

Mom's van is _____.   ◯ little   ◯ big

Where do we go in the van?   ◯ school   ◯ home

How many kids can fit in the van?   ◯ 5   ◯ 6

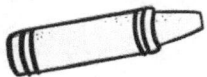

Color mom's van.

Talk About The Text
(Parents, ask your child these questions about the text)

The story says mom's van is big.

How do you know this is true?

I can read about...

Mom And Her Van

Mom has a big blue van.

She can go fast in her van.

Six kids can fit in the van.

We ride to school in moms van.

My name: _____

☆ ☆ ☆

I can read about...

The Hot Day

It is a sunny day.

The sun makes it hot.

Pat does not like to be hot.

He will put on his red cap.

What makes it hot?	◯ the sun	◯ the cap
Does Pat like to be hot?	◯ yes	◯ no
Who will put on a red cap?	◯ Pat	◯ the sun

Color Pat's cap.

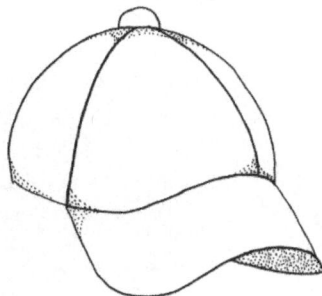

Talk About The Text
(Parents, ask your child these questions about the text)

Why will Pat put on his cap?

Colour a star each time
You read the story.

I can read about...

The Hot Day

It is a sunny day.

The sun makes it hot.

Pat does not like to be hot.

He will put on his red cap.

My name: _____

I can read about...

Max And Dad

Max likes to fish.

His dad likes to fish too.

Max and his dad go to the big lake.

Oh no! The boat will not go!

Who likes to fish?	◯ Mom	◯ Max
The lake is _____.	◯ big	◯ little
Who goes to the lake with Max?	◯ his dad	◯ a pal

Write the word.

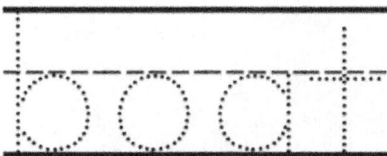

b o a t

Talk About The Text

(Parents, ask your child these questions about the text)

What problem do Max and his dad have?

My name: _____

Color a star each time you read the story.

☆ ☆ ☆

I can read about...

The Big Box

Mom has a big brown box.

What is in the box?

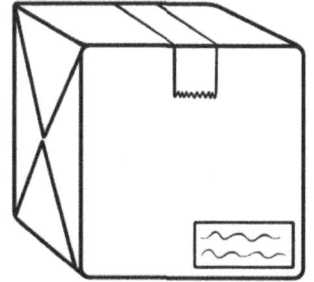

Mom lets me look in the box.

I see a pink pig in the box!

Who has a big box?	◯ mom	◯ a pig
What color is the box?	◯ brown	◯ black
Where do I look?	◯ on the bed	◯ in the box

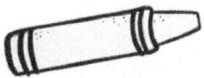

Color the pig.

Talk About The Text
(Parents, ask your child these questions about the text)

Is the pig a surprise?

How do you know?

29

My name: _____

☆ ☆ ☆

I can read about...

Bugs In A Jar

Come see my bugs.

One is big and two are little.

I keep my bugs in a jar.

It is fun to look at bugs.

How many bugs are big?	○ one	○ two
Where are the bugs?	○ in a box	○ in a jar
Looking at bugs is _____	○ fat	○ fun

Write the word.

look

Talk About The Text
(Parents, ask your child these questions about the text)

How many bugs are there in all?

How do you know?

31

My name: _____

I can read about...

Bugs In A Jar

Come see my bugs.

One is big and two are little.

I keep my bugs in a jar.

It is fun to look at bugs.

How many bugs are...?   ○ one   ○ two

Where are the bugs?   ○ in a box   ○ in a jar

My name: _____

☆ ☆ ☆

I can read about...

The Lost Pet

Cam can not find her pet rat.

She is so sad.

Cam looks and looks for it.

Cam finds her rat under the bed.

Who is sad?	◯ dad	◯ Cam
What does Cam look for?	◯ her bed	◯ her rat
Cam finds it under the ____ .	◯ box	◯ bed

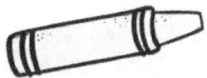

Draw where Cam finds her rat.

Talk About The Text
(Parents, ask your child these questions about the text)

How do you think Cam feels at the end of the story? Why?

My name: _____

Color a star each time
you read the story.

☆ ☆ ☆

I can read about...

Jim and Kim Go Fast

Jim and Kim get in the car.

The car is big and red.

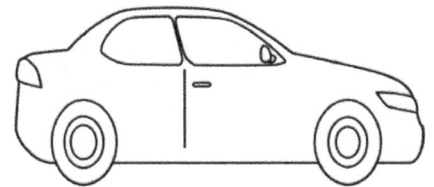

Jim says go. Kim hits the gas.

Jim and Kim go fast! Jim says stop.

What color is the car?	◯ black	◯ red
Who hits the gas?	◯ Jim	◯ Kim
What does Jim say first?	◯ go	◯ stop

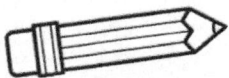

Write
the word.

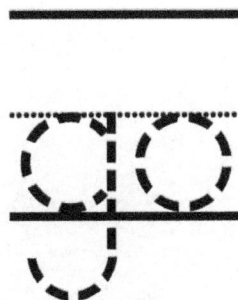

go

Talk About The Text
(Parents, ask your child these questions about the text)

Why do you think Jim said stop?

My name:

I can read about

Jan and Kim Go Fast

Jim and Kim get in the car.

The car is big and red.

Jim says go. Kim hits the gas.

Jim and Kim go fast. Jim says stop.

My name: _____

☆ ☆ ☆

I can read about...

My Kite

I have a kite.

My kite is green and blue.

My kite goes up and up.

I love to fly my kite in the sky.

What do I have?	◯ a cat	◯ a kite
Where does my kite go?	◯ out	◯ up
I fly my kite in the ____ .	◯ house	◯ sky

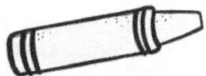

Color the kite.

Talk About The Text
(Parents, ask your child these questions about the text)

Is the boy having fun?

How can you tell?

37

My name: _____

Color a star each time you read the story.

☆ ☆ ☆

I can read about...

A Day At The Zoo

Dan and Sid go to the zoo.

They see a lot of animals.

Dan pets a green snake.

Sid has a hot dog for lunch.

Dan and Sid go to the _____ .	◯ zoo	◯ park
Who pets a snake?	◯ Dan	◯ Sid
What does Sid have for lunch?	◯ pizza	◯ hot dog

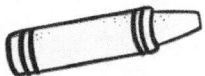

Color the snake.

Talk About The Text
(Parents, ask your child these questions about the text)

Does Dan like snakes?

How can you tell?

39

My name: _____

I can read about...

A Trip To Camp

Ben and Ted are going to camp.

They pack two bags of food.

Ben gets out his blue tent.

Ted says it is time to go.

Who is going to camp with Ted?	○ Bob		○ Ben
What does Ben get?		○ food	○ tent
They pack ___ bags of food.	○ 2		○ 10

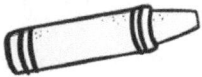

Color the tent.

Talk About The Text
(Parents, ask your child these questions about the text)

Did Ben and Ted pack everything they need? Why do you think that?

41

My name

I can read about.

A Trip to Camp

Ben and Dad are going to camp.

They pack two bags of food.

Ben gets out the blue tent.

Dad says it is time to go.

My name: _____

☆ ☆ ☆

I can read about...

The Nest

Do you see that nest up in the tree?

It has three eggs in it.

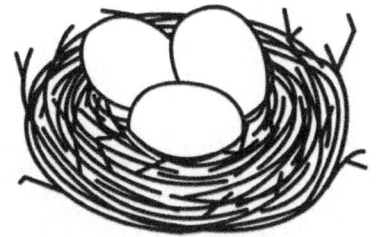

The eggs are white.

A little yellow bird lives in the nest.

What is in the tree?	◯ a bug	◯ a nest
What color are the eggs?	◯ yellow	◯ white
The bird is _____ .	◯ little	◯ funny

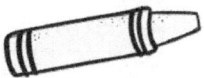

Color the bird.

Talk About The Text
(Parents, ask your child these questions about the text)

Whose eggs are in the nest?

How do you know?

43

My name: _____

I can read about...

The Sun

The sun is up in the sky.

It is a big yellow star.

The sun is made of hot gas.

Do not look at the sun. It is bad for your eyes.

What is the sun?	◯ a rock	◯ a star
Should you look at the sun?	◯ yes	◯ no
What is the sun made of?	◯ gas	◯ gum

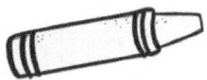

Color
the sun.

Talk About The Text
(Parents, ask your child these questions about the text)

Why shouldn't you look at the sun?

My name: _____

⭐ ⭐ ⭐

I can read about...

A Cake For Me

Mom bakes a cake just for me.

She puts five candles on top.

The cake is yellow.

Yum, it is a good cake!

Who bakes a cake?	◯ me	◯ mom
Is the cake good?	◯ yes	◯ no
How many candles are on top?	◯ 4	◯ 5

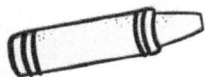

Color the cake.

Talk About The Text
(Parents, ask your child these questions about the text)

Why did mom bake a cake for me?

How can you tell?

My name:

Color a star each time
you read the story.

I can read about...

Cake For Me

When Mom bakes a cake just for me,

She put five candies on top.

The cake is yellow.

There is a lot of...

ANSWER KEYS

My name: _ _ _ _ _ _ _ _ _ _

I can read about...

My Dog Sam

Sam is my dog.

He likes to play.

Sam has a red ball.

He plays with the red ball.

Who is Sam?	◯ my dad	● my dog
What does Sam like to do?	● play	◯ jump
What does Sam play with?	● a ball	◯ a bone

Color Sam's ball.

SHOULD BE COLORED RED

Talk About The Text
(Parents, ask your child these questions about the text)

Is Sam a girl or a boy?

How do you know?

My name: _____

I can read about...

Pam's New Pal

Pam has a new pal.

She met her pal at the park.

Pam and her pal run and play.

Pam's new pal is Jen.

| Where did Pam meet a pal? | ● park | ○ school |

| Who is Pam's pal? | ○ Jim | ● Jen |

| What do Pam and her pal do? | ● run | ○ sit |

Write the word.

park

Talk About The Text
(Parents, ask your child these questions about the text)

Did the pals have fun?

How can you tell?

My name: _____

⭐ ⭐ ⭐

I can read about...

A Hot Pot

That is a very big pot.

I want to look in the pot.

Stop! That pot is too hot!

Mom put the lid back on top.

Where do I want to look? ● in the pot ○ on a lid

The pot is very _____. ○ little ● big

What did mom put on top? ● the lid ○ the pot

Write the word.

stop STOP

Talk About The Text
(Parents, ask your child these questions about the text)

What might have happened if mom didn't say stop?

My name: _____

⭐⭐⭐

I can read about...

My Cat Tab

Tab is my fat black cat.

She likes to sit on the mat.

Tab naps on her mat.

Then Tab will play on the mat.

What is my cat's name?	● Tab	○ Tom
Where does Tab nap?	○ in bed	● on her mat
What kind of cat is Tab?	○ fun	● fat

Color Tab.

SHOULD BE COLORED BLACK

Talk About The Text

(Parents, ask your child these questions about the text)

What happens after Tab naps?

How do you know?

My name: _____

Color a star each time
you read the story.

☆ ☆ ☆

I can read about...

Mom And Her Van

Mom has a big blue van.

She can go fast in her van.

Six kids can fit in the van.

We ride to school in mom's van.

Mom's van is _____.	⚪ little	⚫ big
Where do we go in the van?	⚫ school	⚪ home
How many kids can fit in the van?	⚪ 5	⚫ 6

Color mom's van.

SHOULD BE COLORED BLUE

Talk About The Text
(Parents, ask your child these questions about the text)

The story says mom's van is big.

How do you know this is true?

My name: _____

I can read about...

Color a star each time you read the story.

☆ ☆ ☆

The Hot Day

It is a sunny day.

The sun makes it hot.

Pat does not like to be hot.

He will put on his red cap.

What makes it hot?	● the sun	○ the cap
Does Pat like to be hot?	○ yes	● no
Who will put on a red cap?	● Pat	○ the sun

Color
Pat's cap.

SHOULD BE COLORED RED

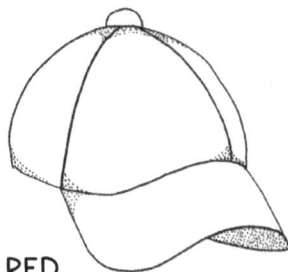

Talk About The Text
(Parents, ask your child these questions about the text)

Why will Pat put on his cap?

My name: _____

Color a star each time
you read the story.

☆ ☆ ☆

I can read about...

Max And Dad

Max likes to fish.

His dad likes to fish too.

Max and his dad go to the big lake.

Oh no! The boat will not go!

Who likes to fish?	○ Mom	● Max
The lake is _____.	● big	○ little
Who goes to the lake with Max?	● his dad	○ a pal

Write the word.

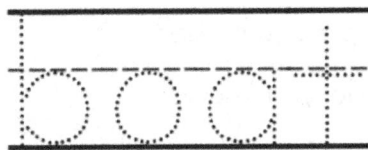

boat

Talk About The Text
(Parents, ask your child these questions about the text)

What problem do Max
and his dad have?

My name: _____

☆ ☆ ☆

I can read about...

The Big Box

Mom has a big brown box.

What is in the box?

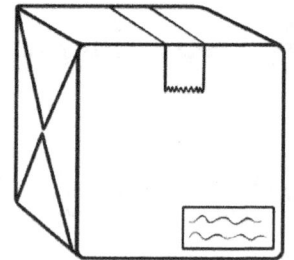

Mom lets me look in the box.

I see a pink pig in the box!

Who has a big box?	● mom	○ a pig
What color is the box?	● brown	○ black
Where do I look?	○ on the bed	● in the box

Color the pig.

SHOULD BE COLORED PINK

Talk About The Text
(Parents, ask your child these questions about the text)

Is the pig a surprise?

How do you know?

My name: _____

I can read about...

Bugs In A Jar

Come see my bugs.

One is big and two are little.

I keep my bugs in a jar.

It is fun to look at bugs.

How many bugs are big?	● one	○ two
Where are the bugs?	○ in a box	● in a jar
Looking at bugs is _____	○ fat	● fun

Write the word.

look

Talk About The Text
(Parents, ask your child these questions about the text)

How many bugs are there in all?

How do you know?

My name: _____

Color a star each time
you read the story.

☆ ☆ ☆

I can read about...

The Lost Pet

Cam can not find her pet rat.

She is so sad.

Cam looks and looks for it.

Cam finds her rat under the bed.

Who is sad?	○ dad	● Cam
What does Cam look for?	○ her bed	● her rat
Cam finds it under the _____ .	○ box	● bed

Draw where Cam finds her rat.

Talk About The Text
(Parents, ask your child these questions about the text)

How do you think Cam feels at the end of the story? Why?

My name: _____

Color a star each time
you read the story.

I can read about...

Jim and Kim Go Fast

Jim and Kim get in the car.

The car is big and red.

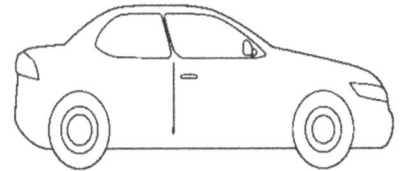

Jim says go. Kim hits the gas.

Jim and Kim go fast! Jim says stop.

What color is the car?	● black	○ red
Who hits the gas?	○ Jim	● Kim
What does Jim say first?	● go	○ stop

Write the word.

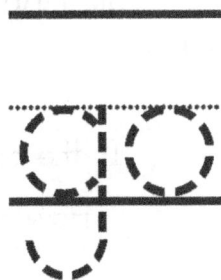

go

Talk About The Text
(Parents, ask your child these questions about the text)

Why do you think Jim said stop?

My name: _____

Color a star each time you read the story.

☆ ☆ ☆

I can read about...

My Kite

I have a kite.

My kite is green and blue.

My kite goes up and up.

I love to fly my kite in the sky.

What do I have?	○ a cat	● a kite
Where does my kite go?	○ out	● up
I fly my kite in the ____ .	○ house	● sky

Color the kite.

SHOULD BE COLORED GREEN AND BLUE

Talk About The Text
(Parents, ask your child these questions about the text)

Is the boy having fun?

How can you tell?

My name: _____

Color a star each time
you read the story.

☆ ☆ ☆

I can read about...

A Day At The Zoo

Dan and Sid go to the zoo.

They see a lot of animals.

Dan pets a green snake.

Sid has a hot dog for lunch.

Dan and Sid go to the _____ .	● zoo	○ park
Who pets a snake?	● Dan	○ Sid
What does Sid have for lunch?	○ pizza	● hot dog

Color
the snake.

SHOULD BE COLORED GREEN

Talk About The Text

(Parents, ask your child these questions about the text)

Does Dan like snakes?

How can you tell?

63

My name: _____

Color a star each time you read the story.

⭐ ⭐ ⭐

I can read about...

A Trip To Camp

Ben and Ted are going to camp.

They pack two bags of food.

Ben gets out his blue tent.

Ted says it is time to go.

Who is going to camp with Ted?	◯ Bob	⬤ Ben
What does Ben get?	◯ food	⬤ tent
They pack ___ bags of food.	⬤ 2	◯ 10

Color the tent.

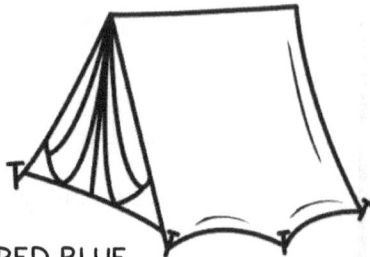

SHOULD BE COLORED BLUE

Talk About The Text
(Parents, ask your child these questions about the text)

Did Ben and Ted pack everything they need? Why do you think that?

My name: _____

Color a star each time
you read the story.

I can read about...

⭐ ⭐ ⭐

The Nest

Do you see that nest up in the tree?

It has three eggs in it.

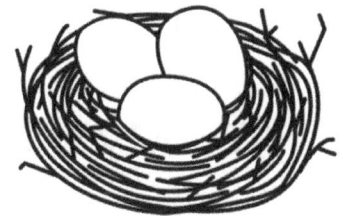

The eggs are white.

A little yellow bird lives in the nest.

What is in the tree?	○ a bug	● a nest
What color are the eggs?	○ yellow	● white
The bird is _____ .	● little	○ funny

Color
the bird.

SHOULD BE COLORED YELLOW

Talk About The Text
(Parents, ask your child these questions about the text)

Whose eggs are in the nest?

How do you know?

My name: _____

☆☆☆

I can read about...

Jim and Kim Go Fast

Jim and Kim get in the car.

The car is big and red.

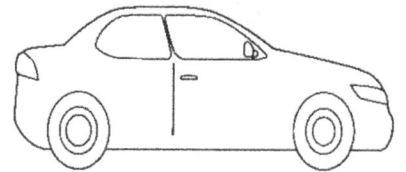

Jim says go. Kim hits the gas.

Jim and Kim go fast! Jim says stop.

What color is the car?	● black	○ red
Who hits the gas?	○ Jim	● Kim
What does Jim say first?	● go	○ stop

Write the word.

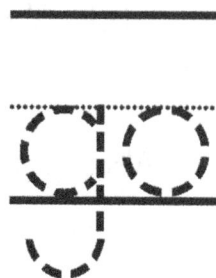

go

Talk About The Text
(Parents, ask your child these questions about the text)

Why do you think Jim said stop?

My name: _____

I can read about...

A Cake For Me

Mom bakes a cake just for me.

She puts five candles on top.

The cake is yellow.

Yum, it is a good cake!

Who bakes a cake?	◯ me	⬤ mom
Is the cake good?	⬤ yes	◯ no
How many candles are on top?	◯ 4	⬤ 5

Color the cake.

SHOULD BE COLORED YELLOW

Talk About The Text
(Parents, ask your child these questions about the text)

Why did mom bake a cake for me?

How can you tell?

Made in the USA
Middletown, DE
06 September 2024